This book belo

D1361899

_____

This book is dedicated to my children - Mikey, Kobe, and Jojo.
May you never stop creating solutions.

978-1-951056-01-8 Printed and bound in the USA. First printing November 2019. GrowGrit.co

Inventor Ninja

By Mary Nhin   Pictures By Jelena Stupar

Can you create a robot
from tape, tubes, and
cardboard boxes?
Inventor Ninja could!

Can you invent things
while you poop?
Inventor Ninja could!

Can you invent while
sleeping?
Inventor Ninja could!

He was the most inventive
Ninja you'll ever meet. And
he lived in Positano, Italy.

When Lazy Ninja was too lazy to wipe his butt, Inventor Ninja created a toilet that washed his butt for him.

When one of Gritty Ninja's legs broke and he couldn't practice his drills anymore,

Inventor Ninja created a special soccer training tool so that Gritty Ninja wouldn't miss a beat.

And when Dishonest Ninja began to tell a lie, Inventor Ninja created a phone app that alerted him of the danger of telling the lie before he could open his mouth.

His light bulb turned off...

All his friends from town gathered around. They talked about what might be the problem and discussed possible solutions.

Lazy Ninja said,

Gritty Ninja said,

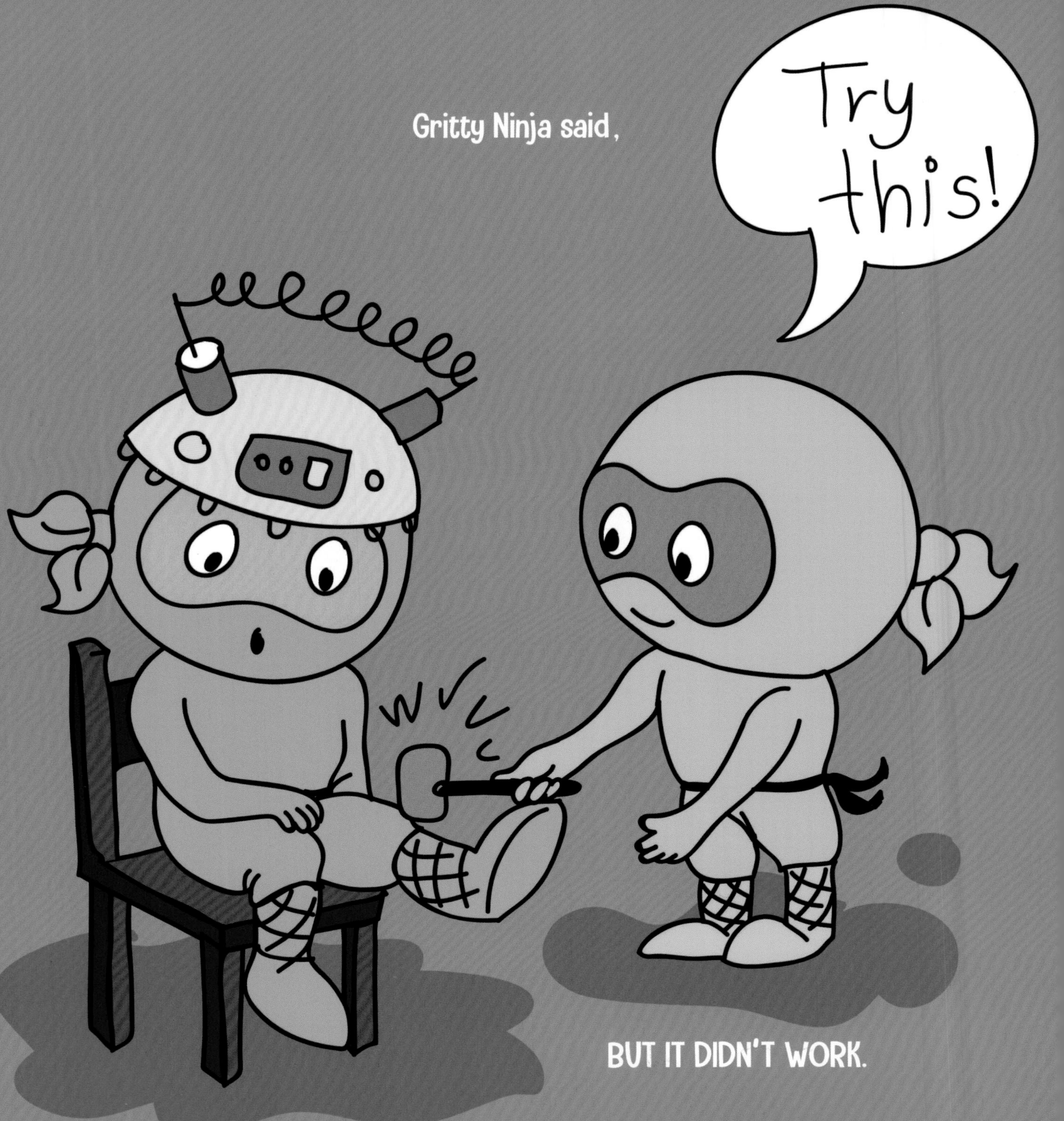

BUT IT DIDN'T WORK.

Then, he heard a knock on the door.

It was Positive Ninja and he had a box with him.

That evening the Ninjas spent time doing absolutely nothing but playing games.

Twister. Checkers. Chess.

They laughed all night!

Then, suddenly one of their favorite games broke...
and do you know what happened next?

Inventor Ninja's light bulb came on and he invented a new way to play it!

If you're ever feeling not so creative, just do something fun to relax. Doing this sets your mind free so it can recharge!

Sign up for new Ninja book releases at GrowGrit.co

:camera: @marynhin   @GrowGrit
#NinjaLifeHacks

:f: Mary Nhin   Grow Grit

:youtube: Grow Grit